Frank Kleinholz-

The Outsider

BY
AUGUST L. FREUNDLICH

UNIVERSITY OF MIAMI PRESS
Coral Gables, Florida

ACKNOWLEDGMENTS

The author and artist wish to acknowledge the assistance of numerous individuals, particularly Mr. and Mrs. Ted Arison, Mr. and Mrs. Norman E. Blankman, Mr. and Mrs. Edward Brown, Mr. and Mrs. Lester L. Doniger, Mr. and Mrs. Eugene Heiman, Mr. and Mrs. Fred Jaraslow, and Mr. Alan Rose.

Contents

Illustrations

Introduction

An unusual figure in contemporary painting is presented by Frank Kleinholz. He is one of a small number of independent artists who do not fit the standard categories. In a period when art runs more than ever to widely pursued styles, and when critical acceptance is more or less dependent upon adherence to one of the favored styles, Kleinholz continues to follow his own path. His stubbornness in being himself has not been lost upon a large number of perceptive viewers for whom originality of expression is more important than a glib notion of up-to-dateness. They know that an artist with a deeply felt outlook is always up-to-date. And Kleinholz' outlook is particularly attractive. It is a joyous, open-armed approach in which his color, paint handling, and pictorial structure are determined by the largeness of his feeling for all that is tender, simple, and vulnerable.

So Kleinholz has the courage to paint subjects that many other able artists hesitate to do because they fear the risk of sentimentality, or because their formal preconceptions demand certain subjects, whether they like those subjects or not. But Klein-

9

holz realizes that sentimentality does not lie in the subjects; it lies in melodramatic or superficial treatment—in falsities and vulgarities of color, paint handling, and interpretation. He therefore has the inner composure to paint subjects that appeal to him, such as flowers, children playing; springtime, birds, city crowds, and homely pastorales, with a zest that comes from full identification with his material. But his gaiety has a subtly disquieting undertone, as if the artist understood all too well the fragile and transitory nature of his subject matter.

Kleinholz' concern with the immediate expression of his feelings is reflected in his spontaneous, painterly style. His drawing is so summary and direct that it verges on rudeness. He wants to get to the heart of things and in the process forgoes the more obvious technical graces. He simplifies drastically, eliminating all elements that do not contribute to the emotional tone he looks for. The result is a personal quality of form and composition which, in their primeval boldness, seem as ancient as they are contemporary. When we add to this apparently unworldly approach to his art the Byzantine splendor of his color, we can see that he springs from the same roots as Chagall and Burliuk. The Slavic inheritance is strong and does not die easily. Clearly, the Brooklyn-born artist has not lost his ancestral memories.

The convincing quality of Kleinholz' work conceals the drastic liberties he takes with the proportions, perspectives, and anatomies of his subjects. Forms are three-dimensional, flat, outlined, or roughly indicated. They are firmly on the ground or they defy gravity. What holds them together is the unity of the outlook, which is unpretentiously humanistic, lyrical, and sometimes fantastic. Thus, in the long run, Kleinholz' art is a product of the imagination, an imagination that is tempered by the tragic realities of life but that resolutely turns to the simple and joyous values we cherish.

JACOB KAINEN
Consultant on Prints and Drawings
National Collection of Fine Arts
Washington, D.C.

Frank Kleinholz-
The Outsider

The Artist in His Present Environment

F rank Kleinholz lives in a development house at the end of a southern Florida street. You drive up the small semicircular drive, go through the large wooden door, see the orchids hanging by the pool, and step into what ought to be the cathedral ceiling living room. But there is no Grand Rapids furniture. The first thing you see is an over-sized Philip Evergood painting. It is a Kleinholz family portrait done in Evergood's fantasy style. Next to it is a beautiful Sudanese mask. Canvases are stacked all about the room, along with a paint table, easels, books, and a few Knoll chairs. This is obviously a painter's studio, but one with a difference. There is only the vaguest hint of life in loft or garret; it is not an opulent place, but it is comfortable as well as artistic.

chapter **1**

A few decades ago Kleinholz captured the essence of the city, to the satisfaction of critics and juries and to the amazement of some artists who, after a lifetime of training, could not believe the validity of an artist who began to paint as a mature person, a lawyer with a secure job and an established non-art centered way of life. Why did he give all this up? What could persuade a logical human being to give up the satisfaction of a desk and an office, a regular nine-to-five schedule, and a substantial monthly income? Kleinholz did at age forty-four, after having developed a passion for creating art. He had been studying part time, gradually spending more time at the easel and less at the desk.

What motivated a man to make such a radical change in his life? What makes any artist paint? One might speak of the urge for creativity and the need for communication, but every human being feels a need to demonstrate his own unique qualities, his difference from his fellows, his superiority in some manner. Most people manage to establish themselves in their own mind's eye as superior or different in one particular way. And for some, their uniqueness becomes unwholesome, not of benefit to society. But for others, the need to be unique takes the more or less dominant form of creative activity—of producing, with great skill, objects that are individually their own production. A painter is such a person. The need to communicate is also a part of the artist's psychological makeup. This is not necessarily a verbal communication or even the communication of anything as tangible as a feeling or an idea. It may be any of these in a work of art, or it may be just a visual concept, but the basis of it is the artist's need to communicate something of his thoughts and feelings.

If this were all there was to becoming an artist, then there would be many more like Kleinholz among us. But most artists are difficult, unusual people. They have idiosyncracies. They have mannerisms and behaviors that sometimes set them apart from society in general and often give rise to outrageous folk myths. We are led to think of the artist as a vainglorious fellow, strutting about like a peacock, asking us to admire his beauty. This artist

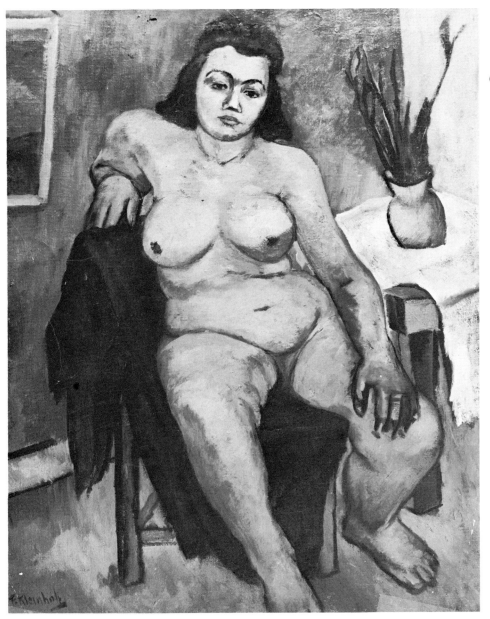

MODEL
1939–40
Oil on canvas
24 x 18
Lost
*(painted at American
Art School)*

15

is, in popular myth, born with his artistic genius and, like all geniuses or near geniuses, is intolerant of the ideas of others. Kleinholz is none of these. Kleinholz is a man who felt the urgency to paint and is devoting the balance of his life to that end. He is a man whose idiosyncracies are expressed through his work.

For some artists there may be something, after all, to that fusty, Victorian concept of the Bohemian life, the notion that the artist must starve and suffer in order to produce great art. Perhaps this kind of notion actually is more than a romantic tale out of the past. Perhaps, though, even in this super-sophisticated, cool, latter part of the twentieth century the inventive individual invents, in addition to his work, a series of defense mechanisms because the world of the ordinary threatens him.

But is Kleinholz such a man? Yes and no. He does not fit the mold precisely. He was not born an artistic genius, he was not threatened by the ordinary. He established himself in a successful career as an attorney before he became involved in art, and when he did turn to art, he went about it in a methodical fashion and did not feel it necessary to give up his comforts. During the last ten years or so, he has lived first in a Long Island suburb and then in southern Florida, because these areas appealed to him and because the way of life possible in these areas made him happy. He is also a settled and devoted family man, and much of his thinking is devoted to the welfare of his wife and children. He collects art and books; he reads, writes, talks, thinks; he is an involved human being.

Kleinholz' vision led him to the art profession by an unusual route. First he became an attorney, successful and comfortable, to all outward views, in his routine. But then, like another earlier professional, Gauguin, he gave up one career to establish himself in another—art. Like the French stockbroker, Kleinholz' art tends to strong and highly personalized statements usually connected with expressionism. It is one of his outstanding aesthetic qualities that he does what he wants to do. It is dogged persistence that has marked him as more than a Sunday painter and has established him as a professional in art, much to the dismay

LEAH
1940
Oil on canvas
40 x 30
*The Sackler
Collections, New York*

BRAVADOES
1944
Oil on masonite
24 x 12
*Senator & Mrs.
William Benton,
Southport, Conn.*

SUNDAY IN THE PARK
1940
Oil on canvas
14 x 11
Lidia Kleinholz

19

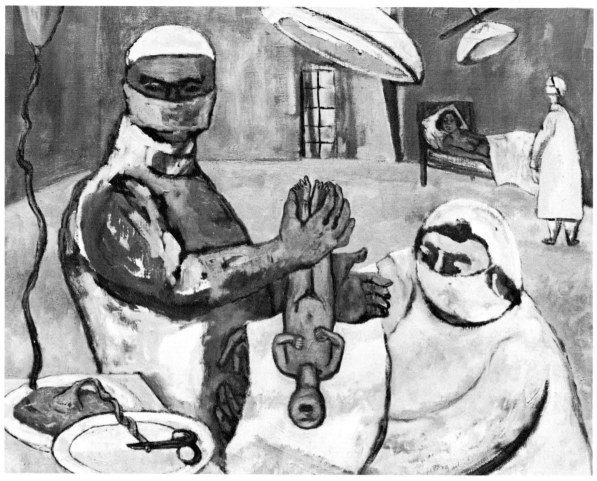

BIRTH
1941
Oil on canvas
24 x 30
Destroyed

of some artists and much to the admiration of many amateurs and art lovers. He has not followed in traditional paths or worked in currently acceptable styles. This personal trait permitted him to give up one career and build another. It is also what has most strongly marked his art.

Kleinholz paintings are characterized by a certain directness and sparsity of detail, an expressionist crudeness. For the artist himself, these factors indicate what he feels are his limitations, some of them imposed by the way a picture begins for him, others

ABSTRACTIONISTS
1941
Oil on canvas
24 x 30
Mr. John O'Connor, Jr.,
Pittsburgh, Pa.

21

by limitations he has not been able to overcome because of his late start as an artist. He feels that he began his work when he was a formed human being. He had never drawn before and yet, within three years, was an exhibiting artist. Since those early days he has worked and studied in many places, driven by the need to overcome his self-found problems. Kleinholz, while developing an integral style, has never chosen and remained with one source of inspiration. He has conformed to the established pattern only partially, by developing his own natural idiom. He refuses to fit the mold and stick to one area of inspiration or to one subject. His technique varies, depending on his interests and requirements.

Although today he is far removed physically from the city and in time from his colleagues in the New York of the early forties, Kleinholz continues in the life he began when he finally left his law office. His comments on life have taken on some of the sunshine of southern Florida, and his subject matter more and more tends to involve children and young people. Over the years his idiom has become more personalized and mature, but basically Kleinholz is still his own man, a maverick among artists.

The Artist's History

Frank Kleinholz has always felt himself isolated from his world. Not that he has been a rebel—he has simply chosen and proceeded along his own path. As a friendly wanderer along life's way, he comments, he looks, and he reacts, a kindly but observant passerby.

He was born on February 17, 1901, in the Williamsburg district of Brooklyn. For many years, as a boy, he guided his blind father about their tenement neighborhood, telling him what there was to be seen and consequently learning to sharpen his own visual experiences. In return, the blind man gave his son, through his comments and reactions, a warm respect for the teeming humanity of their crowded and mixed environment and of his own heritage. While World War I was ending, he was a student at

chapter **2**

Public School #36 with his sister Ruth, and almost as soon as he could count, he was selling newspapers and running errands as a delivery boy to help with the family finances.

In 1916 he entered Eastern District High School in night classes, and after a year attended Eron Preparatory School and the Bedford Y.M.C.A. night school. His mother supported her tribe by running a delicatessen, and Frank continued to help the family with various kinds of jobs. Through one of his instructors at the "Y," Frank was able to secure a work scholarship to Colby College in Maine. With the approval of his parents and an insatia-

CITY CARNIVAL
1942
Oil on canvas
20 x 24
The Phillips Collection,
Washington, D.C.

BACK STREET
1942
Oil on canvas
30 x 40
*Metropolitan
Museum
of Art*

ble appetite for learning, he was sent off to an alien New England world in the fall of 1919. At the college he worked as a furnace tender to help pay for his board and room. After a successful year, which opened up whole new areas of learning, Frank returned home determined to help his family and to become an attorney.

Throughout his adolescence and early manhood, Kleinholz read and wrote, and for years he thought of himself as a poet and writer. While mostly unsuccessful at this endeavor, he continued to write, walk, philosophize with young friends with similar literary, dramatic, or artistic aspirations, and to search for the special role that life might hold for him.

He entered Fordham Law School in afternoon and evening

25

sessions in 1920. In 1923, having worked his way through law school, he was admitted to the New York Bar. As a young attorney with the New York State Insurance Fund, he met and married Leah Schwartz. The young couple soon settled into the life of the professional, with work, bridge, golf, and parties filling their lives. They adopted a well recognized routine; Frank worked in his office and his young wife taught in the New York public schools. It was probably his dissatisfaction with this uncreative routine that was responsible for Kleinholz' career in art. It was a search for a more meaningful and valid off-duty activity that led Kleinholz from bridge and golf first into the study of the piano and finally into painting.

It was through his friends Kay Kinzler and Maxwell Sackheim, who knew of his budding interest in art, that Frank first met Alexander Dobkin, a painter and teacher. Because of Dobkin's interest and encouragement, the Frank Kleinholz family moved to West Sixteenth street in Manhattan so that they might be closer to the art world of Greenwich Village. As the friendship with Dobkin ripened, Kleinholz began to study with him. After a number of months, at Dobkin's recommendation, Kleinholz changed teachers and studied with Yasuo Kuniyoshi.

In 1939 the American Art School announced a scholarship competition in which Kleinholz entered two paintings. He won, and the next year he studied at the school with Sol Wilson as his instructor. While still studying, he was chosen by the faculty of the school for a joint exhibition with a fellow student. One of the paintings in this show, "Sunday in the Park" (p. 19), completed in 1940, marks the beginning of the unique style which Kleinholz has continued to develop.

Now, with the help and kind guidance of Sol Wilson, Kleinholz moved into a large studio apartment in Greenwich Village. It had formerly been occupied by George Kleinsinger, who was off at war. Kleinholz continued his work as an attorney, but painted evenings, weekends, and vacations. He began to meet and become friends with many of the important painters in New York at that time, among them Moses and Raphael Soyer, Bur-

liuk, Gropper, Tchacbasov, Evergood, Gwathmey, and Refregier. Among others whom the artist acknowledges as being among the first to recognize his talents, encourage him, and open doors for him are Mildred Constantine, now with the Museum of Modern Art, and Alfredo Valenti, now with the Gallery of Modern Art. Part of a summer in Mexico next helped the artist to get acquainted with the works of Rivera, Siqueiros, and Orozco.

Nineteen forty-one was a year of change. It was the year Kleinholz submitted the painting "Abstractionists" (p. 21) to the exhibition "Directions in American Painting" at the Carnegie In-

BARGAIN COUNTER
1943
Oil on canvas
30 x 36
Private Collection

THE NAME IS WALKOWITZ
1943
Oil on canvas
20 x 24
*The Newark
Museum,
Newark, N.J.*

stitute. This picture was one of 302 accepted from a total of nearly 5,000 pictures submitted. It was his first entrance into a national exhibition, and it won honorable mention for the until-then unknown painter. "Abstractionists" was chosen by Forbes Watson to be part of a traveling exhibition of the Carnegie show, and the painting was later acquired by John O'Connor, Jr., the acting director of the Carnegie Institute, Department of Fine Arts, for his personal collection. Frank Kleinholz was becoming less a full time lawyer and more a professional painter. In 1942 Reeves

Lewenthal of Associated American Artists Gallery asked him to join its roster and launched him with a one-man show.

The same year, Duncan Phillips of the Phillips Gallery in Washington, D.C. also offered Kleinholz a one-man show, and the Metropolitan Museum of Art in its "Artists for Victory" exhibition included "Back Street" (p. 25) and "Bargain Counter" (p. 28). "Back Street" was acquired for the museum's permanent collection. Among the other winners in the competition were John Steuart Curry, Jack Levine, Marsden Hartley, Alexander Calder, Philip Evergood, Jacob Lawrence, and Mark Tobey. *Newsweek*, in commenting on Kleinholz' work, called him "the Brooklyn-born Gauguin."

In 1943 Kleinholz' paintings were seen in the Whitney Museum Annual Exhibition at the Chicago Art Institute, and again at the Carnegie Institute. He was elected a member of the American Group, Inc., and through the assistance of the late Francis Henry Taylor, director of the Metropolitan Museum, was appointed as a teacher of painting for trade union members' classes that the Metropolitan sponsored that year.

Nineteen forty-four was a year of numerous exhibitions and the start of a weekly radio series over station WNYC. On this radio program, which lasted for one year, Kleinholz interviewed the figures of New York's art world, often stirring up considerable interest and controversy. Among his exhibitions were "One Hundred Artists and Walkowitz," in which he showed "The Name is Walkowitz" (p. 29), at the Brooklyn Museum; "Pathways Through Art 1944," an American Group show; "Portrait of America" at the Metropolitan Museum; and "Painting in the U.S.A." at the Carnegie Institute.

After a long and terrible illness, Leah Kleinholz died of cancer in November of 1945. Shortly thereafter, Frank left his position with the State Insurance Fund to devote his life to painting. He continued to paint, exhibit, lecture, and teach. In 1946 he was again in the Whitney Annual, in the Pennsylvania Academy Biannual, at the Carnegie, and in the Springfield, Massachusetts, Museum Annual exhibitions. He also began to teach a class for the Brooklyn Museum.

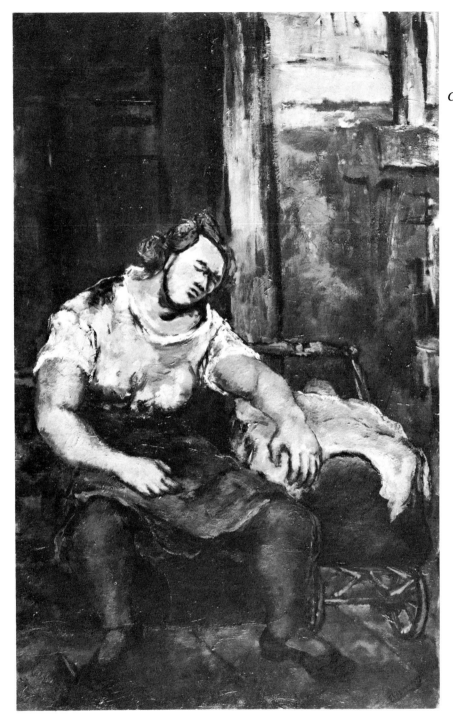

SIESTA
1943
Oil on masonite
30 x 18
*The Joseph H.
Hirshhorn
Collection, New York*

It was during this time that he became affiliated with the Encyclopedia Britannica Collection of Contemporary American Painting as a member of their Art Advisory Board. The directors of the encyclopedia assembled this important collection of contemporary American painting, exhibited it throughout the United States, and published it in book form. The painting "Bravadoes" (p. 18) was purchased for this collection. It is now in the collection of Senator and Mrs. William Benton.

A Quaker schoolteacher, Lidia Brestovan, became the second Mrs. Kleinholz in 1946, and their first child Lisa was born the following year. Lidia has been a strong influence in shaping Frank's life. It was her support and encouragement that made it possible for Frank to continue to paint full time, first through her own interest in art and second through her willingness to help support their family.

By 1948 Frank Kleinholz had been exhibiting for eight years as a professional artist, with six one-man shows to his credit and participation and prizes in important national shows. He had "arrived"—he was an established "successful" artist. Yet, he felt the lack of years of study, practice, and technical training. It was for this reason that in September, 1948, the Kleinholz family sailed for France, where Frank felt sure he could concentrate on the missing elements he needed.

Upon their arrival in France, Joseph Floch, a colleague from the Associated American Artists Gallery, rented Frank his studio on the Avenue de Chatillion. For living quarters for the family, Lidia traded a silver fox cape that had been given to her by an aunt for a flat in the Rue Mademoiselle. Along with the colony of new expatriates, G.I.'s, and old friends, Kleinholz studied art, drawing in life classes at the Grand Chaumière, in the streets, and sketching the people of Paris. For almost two years Kleinholz lived the traditional artist's life in France, studying, drawing, painting; learning the techniques of lithography, etching, and woodcut; and traveling around Europe to visit museums and architectural landmarks. A son, Marco, was born in 1950.

In late 1950 he returned to the United States with his family,

FACTORY GATE
1943
Oil on canvas
40 x 30
Lidia Kleinholz

and bought a house in Lidia's home town, Port Washington, on the far end of Long Island. A third child, Anna, was born in 1959. After setting up his new studio, he started adult painting classes, which quickly filled up. Shortly thereafter, he was engaged as an instructor of fine arts at Hofstra College in Hempstead, New York. April of 1951 saw the resumption of his series of one-man

33

SHOPPING ON AVENUE A
1943–44
Oil on canvas
36 x 24
Mr. & Mrs. Edward
Weiss

34

A NEW BABY COMES TO OUR NEIGHBORHOOD
1954
Oil on canvas
30 x 50
Mr. & Mrs. Norman E. Blankman,
Sands Point, New York

35

THE "A" TRAIN
1955
Oil on canvas
24 x 30
Mr. & Mrs. Melvin Sirow,
Kenilworth, N.Y.

36

MRS. SMITH'S CHERRY TREE
1957
Oil on canvas
30 x 18
Mr. & Mrs. Lester Doniger,
Kenilworth, N.Y.

37

RED HEAD
1958
Oil on masonite
26 x 19½
Mr. & Mrs.
Bert Green,
Akron, Ohio

HOUSING PROJECT
1944
Oil on canvas
30 x 40
*The Akron Institute,
Akron, Ohio*

shows at the AAA Gallery. In addition, he won a purchase prize in graphics at Syracuse University, and he showed in museums in Chicago and elsewhere in this country. The State of Israel acquired his painting "Close of Day" in 1952, and also in that year he was invited to participate in the "University of Illinois Annual Exhibition of American Painting."

When in 1955 Hofstra College failed to renew his teaching contract, Kleinholz closed his house, packed up Lidia and the children, and started out on a cross-country trip to exhibit and paint. He was aiming eventually for Los Angeles, but the family made stops along the way in Detroit, where he had an exhibit at the Associated Gallery of Art, and in Chicago, where he rented a suite

39

FRIDAY FISH
1944
Oil on canvas
24 x 34
Mr. & Mrs.
Mischa Kallis,
Los Angeles, Calif.

of rooms at the North Park Hotel and had a successful one-man show. Mr. and Mrs. Joseph Antonow, who were among the people attending the Chicago show, were particularly taken by his work, and they commissioned Frank to do a large mural for a wall in their home. He decided on a triptych to match the Renaissance decor of the room and agreed to complete the mural and return with it during the following year. This large painting, "Apple Tree, Apple Tree" (p. 71), is now in the permanent collection of Marquette University in Wisconsin. The Kleinholzes completed their trip westward and spent a number of months in Los Angeles, where Frank painted and lectured, before returning to Port Washington in 1956.

A major commission for the artist in 1958 was a mural for

40

THEY WERE PARTISANS
1944
Oil on canvas
30 x 18
*Kleinholz Family
Collection*

41

AUTOBIOGRAPHY #1
1945
Oil on canvas
72 x 48
*Nassau
Community College,
Garden City, N.Y.*

the entrance to the Sands Point Wild Life Preserve in conjunction with sculptor Alfred van Loen (p. 80); this work was sponsored by the Blankman Foundation. The next three years, 1959 through 1961, were occupied with over forty exhibits and one-man shows around and outside the United States. In conjunction with a

FISH
1946
Oil on canvas
40 x 60
*The Sackler
Collections,
New York*

group exhibit in the Soviet Union, the Moscow Museum of Fine Arts purchased a print, "Boy and Bird" (p. 73), for their collection. The same print was subsequently used by UNICEF for its illustrated engagement calendar and its catalogue.

In 1962 the newly built White Winrock Hotel in Albuquerque, New Mexico, commissioned a series of 120 prints of twelve different subjects to be placed in the guest rooms. During the year 1964 Kleinholz also completed his autobiography, *Frank Kleinholz: A Self Portrait*, which was published by Shorewood Publishers, Inc. of New York. On February 15, Kleinholz had a one-man exhibit at the ACA Gallery in New York. The show opened in conjunction with the publication of his book. In 1965 the Akron Art Institute acquired "Housing Project" (p. 39) for its permanent collection and gave the artist a one-man show. Kleinholz also had an exhibit at the ACA Gallery in Rome and traveled to Italy for the event.

43

DAY'S END
1947
Oil on canvas
20 x 30
Mr. & Mrs. Francis Dekoven,
Miami Beach, Fla.

Since 1967 Kleinholz and his family have lived in southern Florida. He has continued to paint, exhibit, speak, teach, and to hold exhibits at the ACA, his major gallery. He also exhibits frequently at Galerie 99 in Miami Beach. His sometime alma mater, Colby College, awarded him an honorary doctorate in 1968.

Kleinholz continues to paint and make prints in his Florida home, driven by the sure knowledge that no artist can ever exhaust his need to create. For Frank Kleinholz there is no end to the development of the many ideas that are constantly occurring to remind him of his creative legacy.

45

The Artist and His Colleagues

I n fairly rapid order, Frank Kleinholz mastered those achievements that mark a painter as an established professional. He studied with good teachers, exhibited in competitions, won prizes, and was received and shown by commercial galleries. He has acknowledged the influence of other painters on his own work, but he has always been his own man. He has not been willing to follow the dictates of the latest styles accepted by the public or critics. He has, in fact, always been an outsider to the art world, and this is his great strength; he stands out among his contemporaries as one of those artists who persistently has followed his own direction and developed his own style. He has been a friend of many important American artists, but he has never quite been a member of the "in" group—the art world.

chapter **3**

The term "art world" is a concept with many different shades of meaning. For the average citizen, it is *la vie bohème,* an aggregation of types sporting beards and curly hair. For the avid collector of art, it is a series of shops and galleries along New York's Fifty-seventh Street and Madison Avenue. For the young man about to receive his Master of Fine Arts, it is an East Side loft. More than anything else, however, it is a group of artists, critics, dealers, and collectors who at some given moment are the most fashionable and wield the most aesthetic and financial power; in other words, it is the establishment. Kleinholz has been well known by the art world since the late thirties and is, in fact, involved in many of the ideas held by some of its members.

Membership in the art world depends on almost indefinable qualities. Obviously a major qualification is success. Painters whose works do not receive the blessing of sales in the market need not think of belonging, nor do critics whose writings are not published. Geographic location is also important. Iowa City, although the home of a large and important art school, prevents ready participation in art world affairs (unless one has the powerful success of a Mauricio Lazansky). In part membership depends on working in the currently acceptable style or styles, in part it depends on associating with "in" people, in part on having the right people admire your work, and in part is indefinable. It is the indefinable, however, that is most important.

There are many successful artists who are outsiders. They have the wrong geographic location or social origin, or they are shown by the wrong dealers or museums. Whatever the cause, the art world regards them with more than its normal amount of hostility and skepticism. The world of art is visibly competitive and has its share of cutthroats among its producers, purveyors, and commentators.

The work of artists not "in" at any moment may be commented on in less important journals, or given less space and fainter praise, or their work may be purchased but appear in the wrong collections. But more than anything else, their work usually does not fit the currently accepted norm. Perhaps the current

49

STUDIO CORNER
1948
Pen and ink
20 x 24
*Collection
of the Artist*

"out" artists were the fashionable movers and shakers last year or a few decades back.

Kleinholz the artist can never be "in." He is too independent and has the wrong kind of history. No matter what his acclaim, his legal background is a strong disability, perhaps because one feature of today's society is the vast number of Sunday painters— white collar workers and professional people—who seek relaxation in creative work but who cannot be considered, by the wildest stretch of the imagination, competent artists.

In addition to his legal background and late beginning, Kleinholz also is a painter whose idiomatic relatives have been on the wane during the last twenty years, a period during which his mature style developed strength and significance. The artists

FISHERMEN
1949
Oil on canvas
16 x 13
Lidia Kleinholz

51

SKETCH FOR PIGALLE
1949–50
Collection of the Artist

SKETCH FOR PIGALLE
1949–50
Collection of the Artist

52

who have most strongly influenced his style have also become his
close friends. He met them as he started painting in the New York
of the forties. Among his teachers, the first, Alexander Dobkin,
became his chief mentor. At the time Kleinholz first started studying with him Dobkin had been on the faculty at Columbia University and was, in the early forties, involved with the WPA art
project. Dobkin had grown up under the tyranny of Cezanne's
concern for drawing. Kleinholz' first drawings, done under Dobkin and since lost, were precise abstractions. The master soon
realized that his pupil had an excellent feeling for paint and urged
him to devote more time and intense study to painting. After a
number of months and while their friendship ripened, Dobkin

53

recommended that it was time for Kleinholz to study with some-
one else, and so he studied next with Kuniyoshi, who was then
teaching at the New School.

Kleinholz' next important teacher was Sol Wilson, with the
American Art School on Fourteenth Street. The faculty and students here comprised an idealistic group. The school, an out-
growth of the John Reed Club, was attempting to make a change
in the education of artists. The group wanted to eliminate the
near obligation on the part of the teacher to please the student
who paid the fees that sustained the faculty. Support for the
school's endeavor came through contributions from many
sources, both from artists and well-to-do patrons. On the faculty,

BUSY CORNER
1958
Oil on masonite
16 x 24
*Mr. & Mrs. Eugene C. Heiman,
Coral Gables, Fla.*

PORTRAIT OF RITA DONIGER
1960
Oil on canvas
24 x 18
Mr. & Mrs. Lester Doniger, Kenilworth, N.Y.

YACHT RACE
1960
Oil on masonite
8½ x 3½
Dr. & Mrs. Allen Berlin,
Detroit, Michigan

58

SKETCH FOR PIGALLE
1949–50
Collection of the Artist

SKETCH FOR PIGALLE
1949–50
Collection of the Artist

PIGALLE
1950
Oil on canvas
30 x 50
*Kleinholz Family
Collection*

in addition to Wilson, were Moses Soyer, Harry Sternberg, Harry Gottlieb, Anton Refregier, and Philip Reisman, among others.

In addition to his teachers, Dobkin, Kuniyoshi, and Wilson, Kleinholz' closest artist friends have been Joseph Hirsch, Robert Gwathmey, Anton Refregier, and Philip Evergood. These men gave Kleinholz artistic acceptance, they viewed his work as professional, and they backed him with psychological support. Kleinholz admires their work, each for its own quality—Hirsch for his great skill as a draftsman, Gwathmey for his elegance of style, and Refregier for his command of mural painting. But of this group, Evergood probably had the greatest meaning and influence on Kleinholz, both as a person and as an artist.

Evergood is of particular significance. He is the *bête noir*, the bad luck and accident-prone friend of many artists; his ideas and style are influential. Of the painting of Kleinholz and his family by Evergood, Kleinholz has said, "It's a personal statement that Philip Evergood made about my family and myself,

MARCO AS
INDIAN CHIEF
1954
Oil on masonite
30 x 19
A.C.A. Gallery,
New York

and I think it's a wonderful portrait. I know it's me, and I know the woman in it is my wife, and so forth. I like the way he constructed the thing. It's a very individual thing the way he put the chair in. Nobody ever saw a sofa that was that color and that shape. This is an Evergood sofa and shape. See that mask? See the way it came out there? It's completely different. In other words, it's an African mask made by Evergood. Lidia did not have riding breeches on. She had a skirt on. When he was finished, she had these fantastic riding breeches on. I like that approach."

Kleinholz is not the only painter to acknowledge the importance of Evergood. His ideas and examples of his works appear in

LET'S DANCE
1954
Oil
10 x 8
*Mr. & Mrs.
Ralph Bettelheim,
New York*

63

THE STORY OF HUMPTY DUMPTY
(Triptych)
1955
Oil on canvas
Collection of
Mr. & Mrs. Donald Dawidoff,
Washington, D.C.

(a) Sitting Pretty
24 x 18

the studios and homes of his friends and colleagues. Moses and Raphael Soyer, Jack Levine, William Gropper, Joseph Hirsch, and Robert Gwathmey all own Evergood's work.

Many of this group also admire German expressionists and particularly the work of George Grosz. Grosz spent what was thought of, by many, as a period of decline in the United States. His work of the twenties had established him as a major figure of the German expressionists and a deeply emotional commentator on the social scene. His American work, by contrast, was chiefly pallid. His major contribution in America, however, and that of other strong German expressionists, is only now beginning to be acknowledged. Grosz had a tremendous influence on Kleinholz, who admits to a continuing fascination for his work.

Even though Kleinholz' first influences stemmed indirectly from Cezanne and he did spend several years in France, he admits to only an academic interest in such French painters as Matisse and Gauguin. They are too decorative for his style. The rugged

64

(b) Was He Pushed or Did He Fall?
24 x 30

(c) "X" Marks the Spot
24 x 18

65

simplicity, vital color harmonies, and directness of the Germans are more akin to Kleinholz' mature work. He feels a particular affinity to such artists as Nolde, Lehmbruck, Kirchner, and Pechstein and likens their biting approach on the social scene to Eugene O'Neill's *The Hairy Ape*. These influences, which began during the artist's maturing period, continue to be seen in his later and present work in which he, like other Americans, has translated into American idiom the traditions of the Germans of the twenties.

These German artists are recognized as having a strong influence in the background of most American social commentary painting. In a sense, the Americans represented a continuation of the philosophy and much of the style of the somewhat earlier Germans. Many of the German group's works are collected by these artists. In Kleinholz' collection appear works by Kirchner, Hofer, Kollwitz, and Grosz as well as such Americans as Evergood, Levine, Moses and Raphael Soyer, and Sloan, among others. In this respect, Kleinholz parallels many social commentators and expressionists at work in this country today who also collect the works of many of the same artists.

Kleinholz, despite his affinities, has never identified with any group. He has many friends and admirers among his fellow artists, but he has always felt himself isolated from the world of art. This probably stems from his late start as an artist and his need to learn from contemporaries of his own age, artists who were already well established in the field. At first, he was much older than most of his fellow students. Later, in Paris, he was a foreigner. It was in Paris, however, that he learned to see a great deal with a new freshness. Because of the newness of the subject matter, he developed an acute visual awareness of it, and the whole experience there sharpened his empathic response to the environment.

Frank Kleinholz has developed a strong and personal idiom with which he charms the viewer into accepting his omissions and commissions. He stands out among his artist friends deliberately and gladly.

An Analysis
of the Artist's Work

Style, followed by content and color, is basic to the painting of Frank Kleinholz. There can be no denying that his work is also mainly American, if for no other reason than its subject matter. His concern with the city and its effects on city people clearly marks him as an American painter of the New York school of the 1940's and early 1950's. It was the city that first concerned him as an artist and its was the city where he had his first success. His views of the city and its inhabitants are his strongest early works. He grew up in the environment of the city; it has permeated his aesthetic soul and comes out of his pictures.

His paintings do not, however, take on the gray and washed-out colors of dark, dingy walls but, rather, reflect the gaiety that he may find in a family wash strung out on an alley line. Where

chapter **4**

another artist might see only the oppressive shapes of buildings, Kleinholz relates to the people, to the warm human life that exists everywhere. He finds color on the fire escape, in the girders of a bridge, in the balloons of children in a park, or in pigeons flying from a rooftop roost. His outlook is not that of the serious social protester; rather, he searches for the lighthearted way to make a serious point. He is not one to look with alarm, though often he is concerned with important issues—the pill, the bomb, and refugees are three topics that have been recent subjects of his paintings. Basically, however, Kleinholz was never at home with the social comment of the American thirties. He was influenced by it through his teachers and through the artists he admired. His own background in the tenements led him at first in this direction, but he has broken out of that mold. He was never much of an alarmist—his nature is too aggressive, his paintings too lighthearted. Perhaps tne groundwork was laid during his year at Colby College, where he first learned about a brighter, greener world that most city youngsters never see. Perhaps also it is due to the perceptions sharpened by his being the eyes for his father, or in the voracious appetite for reading that was also part of his early experience.

The first Kleinholz painting still in existence is a bright and colorful picture that reflects this interest in the brighter side of life. It is a very Cezannesque still life; a group of fruit piled on a table top that has been tilted forward. It is obvious that the tyro has read his art books and has studied the masters thoroughly. There is already evident, however, a looseness of brushwork that speaks of other directions to come.

There are records of many early works in the years 1938 to 1940, but most of the actual pictures have been lost. The existing photographs of such works as "Self-portrait," "Villagers," and "Young Women," all done in 1939, and the one illustrated, "Model" (1939–1940), all indicate a solid kind of drawing in a late expressionist style, well tempered by the then current teaching influences. "Model" (p. 15) is painted well; it might today, thirty years later, still be a promising student's painting that

speaks well of a mastery of such complex problems as drawing foreshortened limbs, developing good value contrasts, or placing a figure into a well-designed composition.

With "Sunday in the Park," "Birth," and other pictures of the years 1940 and 1941, a definite departure in style and maturity of aesthetic judgment are apparent. The mother and child in "Sunday in the Park" (p. 19) are no longer conceived as living models to be caught on canvas. They are now part of the circle of life, an emotional concept expressed in paint. Where "Sunday" is a little heavy-handed in its drawing, "Birth" (p. 20) is complex

69

and refined without being photographic. It is a picture that might have been painted by a follower of Marsden Hartley or Walt Kuhn. It has complex but flattened space patterns and well handled and direct brushwork and drawing.

In the years 1942 to 1945, Kleinholz came as close as he ever did to being involved with social commentary as a style. Illustrated here are a number of typical works with this attitude: "Gossips" (p. 27); "Back Street" (p. 25); "Bargain Counter" (p. 28); "Siesta" (p. 31); "Shopping on Avenue A" (p. 34); "Factory Gate" (p. 33); "Friday Fish" (p. 40); and "Housing Project" (p. 39). All of these compositions, however, speak of life in the city more with a sense of whimsey than with a feeling of protest or condemnation. "They Were Partisans" (p. 41), well received and widely exhibited, lacks the ferocity that the subject demands. It does not involve the viewer directly in a grisly scene but treats us as spectators at a distant event. The corpses of the hanged men are elements in a design rather than men unjustly deprived of life. Kleinholz, although a friend of many of the social comment painters and a man much impressed by their work, never found within his own personality the bitterness necessary for successful work in this style.

The work completed after his return to America began to show the development of the mature style with which Kleinholz has established himself as his own man. Here are found the bright palette, the black outline, the sparse drawing freely applied. Typical are such works as "A New Baby Comes to our Neighborhood" (p. 35); "The 'A' Train" (p. 36), and "Yacht Race" (p. 58).

For Kleinholz the painter, style is the man. It is in all of his work: an honest style, not something put on like a coat, not merely an ancestral or intellectual pursuit. It has evolved over the years as something natural and personal. There are many eclectics, people with facility and great skill. They have formed the coterie of art and are often its best forgers. They can take the work of a Grosz or a Matisse and develop an amalgamation that is commercially acceptable, but transparently not personal. Many painters follow the fashions of the day and are engulfed when the

APPLE TREE, APPLE TREE
(Triptych)
1956
Oil on masonite
82 x 54 closed
82 x 110 open
*Marquette University
Art Collection,
Milwaukee, Wisconsin*

71

mood of the moment changes. They belong briefly to the establishment, but are soon swallowed and disappear because of their lack of conviction, which, like bad underpainting, eventually comes through.

Kleinholz has developed his strengths and has worked knowingly with his handicaps. Somewhere between these two extremes he has expressed a personality in paint. It is a kind of handwriting which marks the mature professional work of an honest painter. It shows in his way of handling a brush, his choice of color and subject.

Kleinholz finds many sources from which his ideas for works of art arise. From his early environment, the city, have come his earliest successes. From his family life, later, have come works concerning children, people, and happier scenes. From his reading of literature and news media often have come whimsical comments. And from other works of art he has acknowledged the importance of his friends and teachers.

Although he has not now lived in the city for some time, the artist feels, as do most critics, that he has rendered the city in a fascinating way, different from any other painter. He has a romantic feeling for the relationship between buildings and people, for structures and movement, which he manages to capture accurately without being specific. Many artists have painted the streets of New York, Paris, or London, but few have captured the human warmth as Kleinholz has. His first important painting, shown at the Carnegie Institute in 1941, is such a picture. The gutter urchins making designs on tenement walls are not mere echos of a bleak childhood, but are warm affirmations of humanity. "Back Street," "Gossips," and "Friday Fish," among others, all echo the same feelings. Many pictures of the city in its various moods and tempos are in existence. Those reproduced here are among the typical treatments by Kleinholz in his best known subject area.

Among the few treating the geometric elements of buildings, "Housing Project" (p. 39), "Day's End" (p. 44), and "Moon Over Bleecker Street" (p. 93), are outstanding. "Moon Over Bleecker

BOY AND BIRD
1956
Serigraph
24 x 36
*Collection of
the Artist*

Street" is particularly noteworthy for the gothic appearance of
mid-twentieth century Manhattan. This, however, is not the artist's preferred content. Kleinholz is not at home with geometrics,
and he takes liberties with what in structure must be vertical and
horizontal. He needs the softness of humanity, not ninety-degree
angles of steel. His paintings of the city are most successful when
they show human situations played against geometrics.

Such paintings as "Lidia" (p. 83), "A New Baby Comes to
Our Neighborhood" (p. 35), "Marco as Indian Chief" (p. 62), and
"Apple Tree, Apple Tree" (p. 71) mark the later reflections of the
artist's departure to suburbia and a growing understanding of
family life. This source has given his work a more happy and
decorative quality that reflects these new concerns. Although

these interests result from the increasingly domestic life provided by Lidia and their three children, it can also be argued that the tendency to explore warm human relations has been present in Kleinholz' painting from its early days. At any rate, as his work matures, the city becomes a backdrop for gentle dramas of mothers, children, and lovers reflected in such works as "A New Baby Comes to Our Neighborhood," "Humpty Dumpty," "Apple Tree, Apple Tree," and even "Yacht Race" (p. 58).

The painting "Birds Gotta Fly" (p. 45) grew partly from a Gershwin song in which the phrase occurs and which was on the artist's mind for some time. It continued to disturb him until one night he woke up remembering the many pigeon coops found on tenement roofs. Pigeon fanciers traditionally bring their birds in with special, long-handled roosting sticks. From these sources, Kleinholz developed sketches of women on rooftops holding pigeon sticks. The objects flying around their head, however, are not pigeons, but children.

Combining current news and other works of art is responsible for another group of paintings. The pope's recent stance on birth control caused a widespread drop in pharmaceutical stocks on Wall Street. The artist for some time had been thinking of human fertility and how it would be affected by "the pill." He also had a fascination about Adam and Eve and the birth of mankind. This led him to search out classical works of art depicting Adam and Eve. He found a painting by Cranach that was of particular interest, and then another by an unknown Florentine artist on the same subject. These two pictures, plus his reaction to them, led to several hundred sketches and a few very small idea paintings. "Homage to the Pill" is a work in progress on which he has worked for a period of several years. In its current state it includes a clipping of the Florentine artist's "Adam and Eve," a fragment of the *Wall Street Journal*, apples clipped from magazine illustrations, and, in paint, a number of references to birth control.

The painting "Pigalle" (p. 60) may serve as a case study of how Kleinholz develops an idea into a finished work. It was be-

THIS IS THE OCEAN
1961
Oil on masonite
10 x 20
Mr. & Mrs. Herbert Grosberg,
Detroit, Michigan

FORBIDDEN FRUIT
1963
Oil on masonite
24 x 52
Mr. & Mrs. Edward Brown,
Oyster Bay, N.Y.

WONDER WHEEL
1963
Oil on canvas
30 x 24
Collection
of the Artist

JAROSLOW FAMILY
PORTRAIT
1966
Oil on canvas
72 x 48
Mr. & Mrs.
Fred Jaroslow,
Manhasset, N.Y.

78

YOUNG ARTISTS
1958
Oil on canvas
30 x 36
Anna Ludmila Kleinholz

gun during the years 1948–1950 when the artist was living in Paris, and the idea was later reworked in several versions. As a stranger to France, Kleinholz was greatly impressed by everything seen. With his sketchbook in hand, he walked around Paris and often settled in the evening at a Left Bank cafe to watch the human traffic. On a Saturday night much of this traffic involves meetings among the young people who frequent this part of the city. From the beginning, the artist was impressed by the importance of the eyes in this game (see sketch, p. 52). They seemed to him to loom very large in the night—reaching out, smiling,

MURAL FOR
SANDS POINT
WILD LIFE PRESERVE
1958
Polyester resin
8' x 20'
Commissioned by
the Blankman
Foundation

suggesting, winking—and these eyes became the focus of the artist's early sketches. An earlier visit to a nudist camp is reflected in the sketches of a milling crowd of nudes (sketch, p. 52). The figure of a little girl is central, surprised by it all, watching her brothers and sisters. The obvious erotic implications also occupied the artist in a number of other sketches (p. 53). Montmartre during daytime is also something of a sideshow with jugglers and magicians. In one sketch Kleinholz shows Picasso at a wheel of fortune (p. 54). In other sketches the artist's attention drifted to close-up views of girls posed in doorways, talking to bartenders or prospective customers. A sketch of the city comes into view as a background for the figures. It is an echo of a work series completed earlier (p. 59). Soon, the ideas blend into final sketches, from which the painting emerged. In it are

CHILDREN'S GAMES
1959
Oil on canvas
20 x 30
*Abbott Laboratories,
Chicago, Ill.*

seen the eye theme, the carnival atmosphere, the city, and the crowd of people, now clothed. Final sketches seek ways of structuring the concept as the painting composition begins to emerge (p. 59).

Kleinholz is not frequently involved in portraits, yet he has done a number of them, as well as family groups, for friends and collectors (p. 56 and p. 78). He is a portraitist who, like Picasso in his famous portrait of Gertrude Stein, is more concerned with catching the essence than the likeness. Kleinholz has a stylistic manner of painting that is so strong that one must recognize first the authorship of the work, then search for the sitter. His portraits have a directness about them that suggests an attack on the canvas with brush and paint, rather than a series of detailed studies and sketches finally culminating in an oil that might be hung in a board of directors' room. The portraits here illustrated show

81

the artist's direct drawing with the brush to establish the figure, with broad areas of color developed simultaneously. Each completed painting has little in the way of a likeness but, rather, has a caricaturish quality with certain aspects reflecting facets of the sitter. Such a picture has much of the expressionist tradition, being the culmination of many experiences, terminating only accidentally in the picture involving a specific subject. For Kleinholz, the photographic eye is too automatic. He has to interpret the sitter's character to develop a feeling for his subject. The sitter might recognize himself, but to Kleinholz resemblance is not a goal. The style of the man is his hallmark. It is most easily identified by the appearance of his visual idiom, rather than the likeness of his subject.

The closest the artist ever comes to real abstraction is when he reacts to arrangements of paint on a random surface. Much in the manner of Gestalt psychology, it is the whole random grouping that acts as a source for knowing the image. Such a method of working has given birth to a series of small paintings made on a wooden palette (see "Self-portrait on a Palette," p. 89). These paintings arose from random play with leftover paint. They have always resolved, however, into a figurative treatment of subject matter in the artist's current interest area.

Other such random activities have come from an interest in collage and pop art enlargements. Kleinholz today is searching for a way of making new statements in the social area by using pop elements. He has, in recent years, frequently used material clipped from magazines as elements in his paintings. Such pictures as "Drummer Boy, Drummer Boy," a painting in progress, reflect this interest. This painting utilizes magazine clippings about the Vietnam war and parts of a plastic toy fighter plane contrasted against a vertically striped painting of red, white, and blue. In the middle stripe stands a small boy in a tricorn, folded-newspaper hat, playing on a drum. The artist's view on the war is obviously negative, but he makes his comment gently, tongue in cheek.

Frank Kleinholz is a lyrical painter of our time, devoting

LIDIA
1962
Oil on masonite
48 x 30
Lidia Kleinholz

through his stylistic idiom the pursuit of his own aesthetics. He has not been a member of the inner working of the art establishment partly because he insists that he will pursue his own ideas in his own way. The creative life he took up at forty-four he now continues as youthfully effervescent as ever.

The Artist
Speaks About His Work

In a taped interview, the artist spoke about his work with the author. The excerpts that follow are arranged out of context to provide a degree of sequence.

The first discussion deals with how Kleinholz approaches his work:

I work on many pictures at the same time because I leave each painting to mature and age like good wine. And the paintings do. I get a chance to look at and study my painting with objectivity. Does it have the qualities I think a good painting should have? Is my original concept coming through? This is the most difficult, for an idea grows and changes. It becomes a variation on a theme and these variations may become concepts in themselves: seeds that grow into other paintings.

chapter 5

I let the layers of paint dry for months and then another layer of paint and perhaps another. If the painting moves too fast, if it comes into being too easily, I get worried about it. I worry about glibness, slickness, over-facility. So I slow up a bit, look at it more carefully. I like to have my concept exceed my capabilities, to challenge me, to make me work harder, to call upon all my faculties, to make me fight and struggle to achieve my ends. It takes much time and energy, but I am rich in time and energy.

There is a great danger in studio painting. It is necessary to work outdoors from life once in a while if for no other reason but to get a breath of fresh air. My pet hate is paintings that have that posed look, that studio look. You can almost see the painter arranging the still life or posing the model. I like a painting— no matter what its origin, to take on a life of its own. I think that is what the word "creative" means. Bosch could paint the wildest imaginative hells and they were real and still are real and terrifying even in an age of doubt and disbelief. The function of an artist is to create life, not to solve mathematical problems.

Before I left for Paris in 1948, I had never painted outdoors. I did paint from life models and still life, but to go outdoors with a paint box, easel, and canvas was something I had never done. The idea intrigued me. I had read about how the impressionists painted outdoors, and though I painted the New York scene I limited myself to making small sketches in my notebook outdoors, and then working from them in my studio. When I got to Paris I found that come the long weekend, painters were out painting in the streets or in the parks or on their way with paint-box hanging from shoulder to paint the countryside. Passersby would hardly stop for a moment to take a hurried glance before moving on.

Gene Grant, a fellow American artist living in Paris at the time, suggested we paint outdoors. We went off to Mantes, outside of Paris, painted in the village square, had a gargantuan

BOARDWALK
1964
Oil on masonite
42 x 24
Collection of the Artist

87

lunch with several bottles of wine, slept away the afternoon under the shade of a tree, and returned to Paris late that night. Recounting the day's exploits to Lidia, I told her that the French knew what they were doing. There was nothing to equal painting in the open, close to nature, seeing her at first hand and translating what one saw to the canvas without any intervening loss of time. Gene and I continued our outdoor work and I enjoyed the experience.

I returned to New York in 1950 and back to the studio I went. Outdoor painting was forgotten. In 1960 I was preparing for an exhibition to be held in Detroit at the Donald Morris Gallery. I decided to center the show around Coney Island and call it "Coney Island, People's Park of Rest and Culture." A reporter from the New York World Telegram *got wind of it and thought it would make a good story. He called me and suggested that I go with him and a news photographer to Coney Island and paint there on Sunday afternoon. I hesitated; it was the height of the summer season and I told him that I'd be mobbed.*

"Nonsense," he assured me, "you won't be noticed."

So off to Coney Island we went—easel, paintbox, canvas, reporter, and photographer. By the time I set up my easel on the beach we were surrounded by hundreds of bathers—young, old, kids, girls in bikinis, muscle men turning somersaults, building human pyramids in front of the cameraman. Kids were crawling between my legs and upsetting my easel, people in the distance were calling "Whatsamatter, somebody drowned?" When the photographer readied his camera there were shouts of "Take my pitcher!" and finally when the photo was taken of me in the middle of the crowd smiling, brush in hand, a kid came up to me and plaintively asked, "Paint my pitcher, Mister?"

That was the only time I tried to paint outdoors in New York. I decided then and there that I would reserve painting from nature for France.

A number of interesting comments were also made about
his methods of drawing and painting.

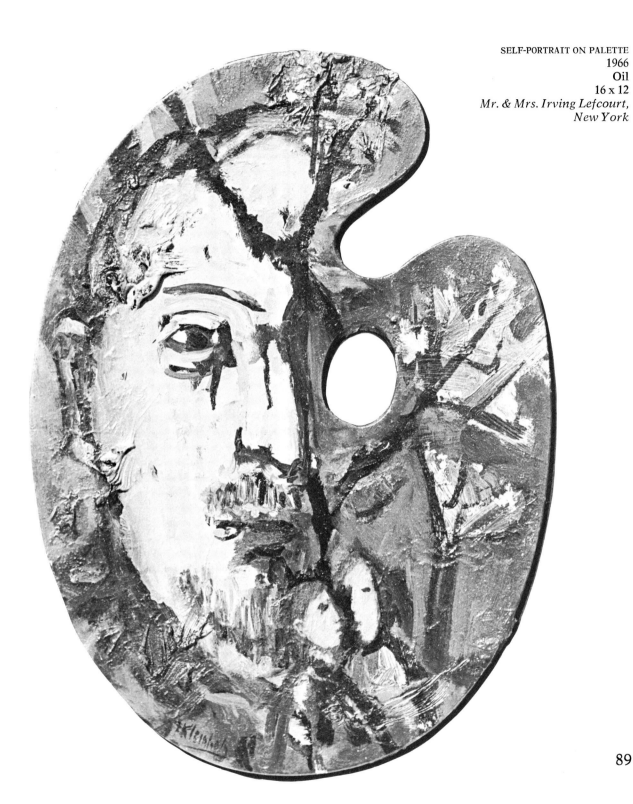

SELF-PORTRAIT ON PALETTE
1966
Oil
16 x 12
Mr. & Mrs. Irving Lefcourt,
New York

89

A good painting has to hold together, have good intrinsic color. All the elements of painting should culminate in expressing my concept.

I rarely start alla prima *on any idea that I believe has some importance and which would justify making a large painting.*

I make many drawings until I can concretize my ideas. Whatever facility I have acquired as a draftsman requires constant work, constant practice no different from that of the concert pianist.

I make numerous sketches, some "quickies," some more detailed than others, until I arrive at one that incorporates everything I want to say in the painting.

I try to interfere as little as possible with paint or color. So I use the simplest method I have been able to find in all the books on techniques of painting from Tratto della pittura *by Leonardo da Vinci to Ralph Mayer. By the way, Ralph Mayer's book is a sort of Bible to me.*
I use the Dutch media, a resin damar based media, one-third damar varnish, one-third sun-thickened linseed oil, one-third turpentine. I use it sparingly. Between layers I use a damar retouch varnish and, finally, damar varnish.

Kleinholz often discusses the struggles of creativity and how they affect both his person and his work.

I have devised a way to both amuse myself and to probe for new variations of color and concept. I just take an empty canvas and throw color at it, looking for happy accidents. When they appear I push them until they take the form that the canvas suggests to me.

I like to fight for my ideas, to struggle to achieve my goals. The tensions, the difficulties in transforming an idea, a vague idea,

HATS
1966
Oil on masonite
16 x 12
Collection of the Artist

91

into the concrete expression of a painting is a struggle I relish and makes painting an echo of life for me.

I am afraid of facility, slickness, shortcuts. I don't like it in other painters and I try to avoid it. I am lucky that I am not blessed with much facility.

I like to think of the number of artists who gave up their secure professions to become painters. Gauguin is the best known —the stockbroker who became a painter. Rousseau was a post office official. Cezanne studied law, as did Matisse. I read that Rembrandt also started as a law student but quickly gave that up to study with a local painter in Leyden.

The law seems to be the profession to run away from. I frequently meet businessmen—lawyers, doctors—who would like to make a change and study art. They ask for my advice and I readily give it. I tell them, "if you want to be a painter don't go to art *school, go to* law *school!"*

About his own life in art Kleinholz is quite direct.

Art, my work, comes first. Everything in my life is subordinated to it. I think, sleep, rest, play, struggle only with art and my work. I love my wife, my children, my home, but my work is really my life and they have become fused with my work. They lead their own lives and where their lives touch mine, it must be to succor and surround me with an understanding and love that shows that they know that art will tolerate no other children, no other loves, no other mistresses.

This they have done, and I must pay a tribute to my dear wife Lidia who has become one with me and my goals, who removes and diminishes the strains and stresses of daily living so that I can work at my best. I am a lucky man. I sell enough to keep the creditors away from the door, and I have the dedication of my wife and children who believe in what I do. Pity the artists whose wives cannot, or will not, understand their work or their way of life.

92

MOON OVER
BLEECKER STREET
1968*
Oil on panel
42 x 28
Mr. & Mrs.
Noah Jacobs,
Lake Success, N.Y.
*original, 27 x 17, painted
1948 and destroyed in
fire; repainted 1968 for
original owners

I have looked at the city differently than any other artist who has painted it. I think I have a feel for people and buildings. I understand what the buildings of the modern city have done to the people who inhabit them. When I showed my painting in my first major competition, it stood out. There were over four thousand paintings submitted to the Carnegie International and only about three hundred accepted

I, a newcomer in the world of art, was accepted! That is difficult today. There are no large, open-juried competitions. But I, and others, had a chance to be seen. Today, after some twenty-five years of painting, people, particularly young people—which pleases me most—love my work and become involved in it. Of course, I try to push a little further in my work. I like the world I created. I don't want to change my fundamental concepts, but I do want to go deeper into it, to express it with greater understanding, warmth, and humanity.

Of course, the greatest moment of my life was walking down the stairs of my studio one morning, opening the letter box, and finding a letter from the Metropolitan Museum of Art telling me that my painting "Back Street" was awarded sixth purchase prize, check for $500.00 enclosed, and the painting was acquired for its permanent collection. I was on my way to work, but I then and there declared a national holiday, returned to my studio upstairs, and sat there stunned until my wife Leah came home from her job.

I greeted her with the words, "Guess what?" . . . Now the trick was no longer to get to the top, but to stay there.

When I finished the painting "Sunday in the Park" I knew I was a painter. Nobody had to tell me. I just knew it. Up to that time I had been floundering around. I could handle paint all right but I didn't know where I was going with it. Every painting I liked, every artist whose work appealed to me influenced me. On Monday, I was an abstract painter, on Tuesday a minor Picasso, on Wednesday an impressionist, and so on. When I did

FLOWERS IN THE
WINDOW
1967
Oil on masonite
36 x 24
Mr. & Mrs.
Ted Arison,
Miami Beach, Fla.

95

WINDY DAY
1967
Oil on masonite
22 x 20
Lisa Kleinholz

"Sunday in the Park" I looked at it the way one looks in the mirror the morning after. Is this really me? Yes, it was. I knew it at first glance, and from that time on I knew I had identity. I knew who I was, what I wanted to do, and where I was going.

The artist discusses his philosophy of art in a deeply intellectual fashion, probing for greater meanings and verbal explanations for what he has accomplished visually.

People, human beings, present the deepest and most challenging subject matter as well as one which is inexhaustible. Why I want to pursue painting and this particular phase of painting is more difficult to answer objectively. I suppose that I engage in this activity because it gives me the completest sense of activity that I have ever experienced. Overall, I am happiest when I work at it. But that, of course, is only a surface answer. Obviously, the artist is motivated by much deeper compulsions, some of which are unknown to him. Frankly, I don't think the deep unknown motivations are so important either to the artist or to the public which enjoys his work. There certainly are many individuals who have all the subconscious motivation to paint but do not paint, and there are those that try to paint and cannot paint no matter how strong their motivation or compulsion may be. There is a catalyst that fuses the many elements that make an artist. Just what that is I do not know and I doubt whether anybody else does—Freud, Jung, and others not excepted.

My ideas come to me most anytime and anywhere. Something I see suggests a painting. At other times a few words will set an idea going. I doodle a great deal, sketching all the time, and some ideas are born that way. I keep a sketch book to which I transfer my ideas and which I use for reference.

For example, the words "Birds Gotta Fly" from Gershwin's song kept floating around in my mind. I kept humming the tune and repeating the words, toying with the idea for months in an attempt to convert it into something visual, a painting. One night between sleep and waking I saw it: many city rooftops, on each a heavy-set woman—the mother image—wielding the bamboo pole that pigeon fanciers exercise their birds with, and in the sky over the rooftops babies flying around like pigeons. I got up, made a few drawings, and started the painting the next morning. It was all there and I did not have to take anything away or add anything.

At other times the canvas becomes a battleground and there is painting and repainting until the thing jells and approaches what I want it to be.

I do not believe in the exclusiveness of the artist. He is a part of society with the same responsibilities as any other member of that society. It is a two-way street despite the fact that at times the very society that made the artist rejects him and fails or refuses to understand him. All the good things in life, and art is one of them, are of greatest importance to all people. What man gets from art depends on many factors: education, tradition, and, you might say exposure to the arts. I believe that art influences and affects man in every facet of life. Sometimes the effects are manifest, sometimes hidden, but they are always present.

There are too many exciting, vital, and positive changes in the making, too many dramatic events shaping. Content is searching for the artist today as never before.

Art is an extension of the man, and like man, changes and develops as man changes and develops. It does not exist apart from man even though once created it may appear to have a life of its own. Like life and reality it does not exist without the existence and consciousness of man. The greatest of art, its profoundest expression, has always been objective, always concerned with man, with humanity, always born out of human experience, always in search of meaning, elucidation, solutions— all subject, of course, to the historical limitations of the period the artist lived in.

I have never done much teaching. Not that I haven't taught at times, particularly when I needed the money. But I think that

THE BRIDGE
1968
Oil
20 x 16
*Mr. & Mrs. Ted Arison,
Miami Beach, Fla.*

99

painting is a full time job and takes all the energy that one has and more. The qualities that make a good painter are not necessarily those that make a good teacher. The reverse is usually true —good teachers can be bad painters and bad painters can be good teachers. Our museums, galleries, art schools, and colleges prove it. They are manned by bad painters masquerading as art teachers, art directors, gallery owners. As soon as a good painter shows that he is a bad teacher he is fired. That is too bad! Good painters should be in the colleges not as teachers but as artists. They should do their thing—paint, talk to students, hold open house once in a while, serve drinks in the studio, and let things happen. I think it would certainly help the situation that newspapers call "student unrest."

When all is said and done it is the artist who supports art, promotes art, defines, understands, and defends art. Not the critic, not the art dealer, not the museum director, not the politician—it is the artist. There are many reasons for this, I suppose not the least being that his survival as an artist depends upon it. But I think that he is first impelled by his love and belief in art as a vital element of life. He will fight for it and for his right to create with freedom. Rembrandt was a great collector of art. It is said that he paid the highest prices for his art treasures, so much so that people expressed surprise. But his answer was that he did it because art must be held in highest esteem.

We have more people painting today than ever before. It seems that everybody wants to get in the act. In this computerized age everyone wants to escape being tagged by a number and pigeonholed. We want to shout to be heard, to create to prove that we are still individuals with identities of our own. And why not—age is no factor. Grandma Moses should be a goal for every elderly person—neither age nor sex stopped her. She needed no art teacher, no art school. The cost of materials is negligible and if one really wants an art school there are night adult courses where tuition is free or nominal. Have I left anything out? Oh

100

yes! Talent! It doesn't hurt to have some talent, but don't let that stand in the way. Look at what people without talent have accomplished. Besides, how does one know what talent one has until he or she tries. Let art ring for everybody. Let's all get into the act—we can use another Rousseau.

Everybody is a critic today. A world full of critics and few artists. They are like the philosophers who Andre Gide wrote about. You ask them a question and you wind up by not understanding the question you asked. They have invented, poor souls, a new language to review, describe, and criticize abstract art. It was a great achievement as important to humanity as Esperanto was—and as dead. Avant garde—what a snobbish phrase! To be ahead of the people. I prefer Carl Sandburg, who believed in the people and wrote "The people yes!" You need no intellectual mediary for Sandburg. He speaks plain and to the heart like all the greats—Whitman, Lincoln, Goya, Shakespeare, Rembrandt.

I think the doctors, the physicians, are the last of the miracle makers. This transplant business is the greatest—a lung here, an eye there, a new kidney for you, a new heart for me, and lo! Lazarus has risen from the dead.

Now, if some doctor could only put some "heart" into the world today—I'm talking about the "heart" that poets write about, remember?—not blood pumps but the "heart" Jimmy Durante sings about when he sings "You gotta have heart!"

Now if some doctor could make that kind of heart transplant that would be the greatest miracle of all.

We should be judged by our peers. Who is to judge the artist, a museum director who has never painted or if he has, has quit, a critic of art, or the artist and his contemporaries? I think the artist is the only one qualified to judge his fellow artists and an end should be put to those juries which have not got a majority of artists on them. Most objectionable is the one-man museum

*director jury. Artists should refuse to submit to this kind of jury.
I think the artist is best qualified to spot the non-artist from the
artist, the amateur from the professional.*

*It is encouraging to see the interest in all the arts today. It
seems that everybody is at it, painting, sculpting, writing, or talking about it.*

*I mean everybody—young and old, teenagers, housewives,
mothers and grandmothers, businessmen, doctors, dentists, lawyers. From every sphere people are rushing to art as a last desper-
ate hope, an escape from the fast enveloping dullness and same-
ness of our computerized world, an attempt to hold on to some
creativity, individuality, in life.*

*This may be the last stand we make against the steamroller
of nonentity, but it is a stand. Don't mow us down! We are individual human beings with the right to exist as individuals, to
sing and laugh and paint and sculpt, make music and poetry and
love! The rock and rollers sing it, the hippies try to live it. Bravo
to them and to me and to all the young. We shall not be overcome!*

*People say they don't like modern art and can't understand
it. Yet it surrounds them and has completely permeated their
lives. The design of women's dresses are lifted straight from
Mondrian. The sets in the TV background are based on abstract
modern sculpture. Our architects have bastardized Frank Lloyd
Wright and LeCorbusier; our ceramists have lifted the forms
from oriental ceramics and bronzes; our plates, cups, table set-
tings owe much to Matisse and Picasso, and our poster art, commercial advertising, and TV commercials don't hesitate to lift
bodily and completely from psychedelic art. And yet they say they
can't see modern art, like it, or understand it!*

*Art is creeping into our daily lives. I saw an advertisement
in the Sunday paper that promised to bring art and culture into
every home—to be more specific, into every kitchen.*

102

The advertisement read something like this: "Thanks to art-

conscious appliance manufacturers, the housewife with artistic taste can now panel her kitchen range door with a Picasso or a Renoir. Your dishwasher, refrigerator, or range could be graced by a Mondrian or a Modigliani."

Pity the poor housewife, art conscious or otherwise, who will try to find art or culture in this way. Art must be revered, respected, and held in high esteem. It is one of the great accomplishments of the human race. There are many places for art in life but certainly its home is in the heart and not on the range.

Finally, Frank Kleinholz discusses his friends and friendships.

Painting is more than putting paint on a canvas. It is a way of life. This is one of the reasons that art cannot be taught. It must be lived. So much of our art today is not lived, not felt, and it looks it. My good fortune was in meeting Alex Dobkin, who kept pushing me out and away from my comfortable and smug thoughts, ways, home, profession, life. Moving from Flatbush to Greenwich Village was a catharsis, a revolution, an upheaval. New insights, new landscapes, new horizons, new friends; music, poetry, painting were the modus vivendi. The things about which life moved —they were the new goals—not as dillettante but as an integral part of every living moment. This was the goal, not some success as an artist, but life *as an artist. This is something the businessman cannot understand. He always asks the same questions; you give him the answers, and then he looks at you with vacant eyes and asks the same questions.*

I like to collect. "Collect" isn't the right word—it smacks too much of acquisitiveness. Put it this way: I like to surround myself with the work of my friends and other artists I admire. I never feel alone and I can always reminisce and talk to them. I've been doing this ever since I studied with Wilson.

I bought my first painting from Wilson—"Across the Tracks" is the title. I still own it, but now it has lots of company:

Burliuks, Raphael and Moses Soyer, George Grosz, and many others; African sculpture, pre-Columbian sculpture. Each one was acquired to mark some important day or event in my life or Lidia's or my children's. I like to buy the work of young artists. Nothing is so encouraging not only to the young but to every creative person as the approval, the approbation of your fellow artist, and when he actually pays real money for the painting the shock is almost too much to bear.

I told you about the collection of art that I gathered from the friends and artists whose work I admired, but I did not tell you about another collection I have—a collection of original poetry written especially for me by a group of handicapped children.

There is on Long Island a school called "The School for Human Abilities," and they employ the handicapped in their establishment. It is one of the most successful schools of its kind, and they asked me if I would speak to a group of handicapped children. I agreed, and on the appointed day I found myself standing before children, some who had never walked, some who had never seen, some who could not use hands or feet, some flat on their backs who could barely move their eyes and heads. I stood there helpless in the face of their difficulties, but they soon put me at ease. They smiled at me—smiles by which they let me in on a secret. They knew that I was one of them, that I too was one of the handicapped, that we all shared this fate in common. I was one of them, accepted and understood, and then it was easy, easy to talk to one's equals.

I spoke of the miracle that was the mind—the human mind that can make song, poetry, pictures; the mind that can fly and can overcome all limitations: space, time, gravity. They liked what I said and so I took advantage of them. I asked each one of them to write a poem and send it to me. They did, and almost to a one they wrote "I can fly." These poems are my own. When I despair, when I feel lonesome, sore at the world, defeated—yes—handicapped, I take them out and read them, and take a flyer with my friends, the weak, the halt, the maimed.

Edwin Alden Jewel, then art critic for the New York Times, *sought me out after my first show and invited me to his home. He said he was curious to meet the man who painted with such maturity and authority with hardly any painting background. He asked me what my plans for the future were and I answered, "to keep on painting."*

"I think you are very good and have lots of talent," he said, "so I am going to tell you a few things that critics usually don't tell artists. You are entering the world of Alice in Wonderland, or, to put it better, Alice in Artland, a strange and weird country inhabited by strange and weird people, most of whom talk about art and don't practice it, painters who don't paint, sculptors who don't sculpt, art dealers who deal from the bottom of the deck all ready to pounce on and exploit and devour anyone who shows talent, integrity. Watch your step, work and then work more, and don't be in a hurry to get there—you are there!"

"Yes, Mr. Jewel," I said, "thank you."

Abraham Walkowitz was one of the sweetest men I had ever known, knowledgable about art and dedicated to it. He wanted to insure his immortality, so he went to a hundred well known artists and had them paint him in any fashion they liked. He planned to have the paintings shown in a large exhibition at the Brooklyn Museum of Art. The show was to be called "One Hundred Artists and Walkowitz."

He asked me to do one of him. I did, and I called the painting "The Name is Walkowitz." It is now in the permanent collection of the Newark Museum. It was recently shown, some 25 years after I had painted it, at the Lowe Art Museum when they gave me a retrospective.

Many people saw the painting and were amused by it. What most did not know was that though I painted a likeness of Walkowitz it really wasn't Walkowitz who was knocking at the Pearly Gates—it was me, myself, announcing my arrival to St. Peter and saying "The Name is Kleinholz."

There is one thing I must mention because it involves a man

I have great respect for—the philosopher Barrows Dunham. He was in Los Angeles at the time I was living there and working in a studio that I shared with Arnie Mesches, Morty Dimondstein, and Marty Lubner. Dunham visited the studio, saw a pastel of mine—a version of "Boy and Bird"—liked it, said so, and it was his. He took it with him and later he wrote me. What he wrote was important to me, of course, but the fact that it was he who wrote it gave me great pride.

"I think I told you," he wrote, "that the picture expresses all my hopes and wishes for the future of mankind. It is wonderful to see how deeply and quickly you have penetrated into the essence of all that matters. I have toiled after it for thirty years of philosophic inquiry, and I find you already there, carried thither in a single flash of an artist's insight."

David Burliuk was not only a great painter, he was a poet, philosopher, a great human being. It was my good fortune to be his close friend since my first show. Emily Genauer wrote a review in the World Telegram *linking our names together. She thought it was disgraceful that I, a newcomer, should have such an immediate success and Burliuk, a painter of many years, not to have received the recognition he deserved. I never could understand what difference it would have made to Burliuk if I had not had a success, but that does not matter now—time has created its own equities. Burliuk, though, felt that this union was made in heaven and saw our careers marching along together. So the review had the wonderful effect of binding us in a friendship that lasted through the years.*

When one thinks of David Burliuk one must also think of his wife Marusha. They were one. She was a great woman in her own right but she subordinated self to nurture his genius. The great love they had for each other ranks with the great loves of history.

He loved parties and would have one at the drop of a hat. An opening, a birthday, an anniversary, the sun was out, it's raining —any reason would do, and we would have a party. As a matter of fact, I met my wife Lidia at one of his parties. Being a lawyer

106

I was supposed to be a "good speaker" and it was usually my function to "say a few words." And a "few words" were what I had plenty of.

At that time he lived on the lower East Side, and I would visit him, ostensibly to help him translate his poetry, which he wrote in Russian, to English. I don't know what qualified me to be a translator, for I knew no Russian and I had never translated anything, let alone Russian poetry. But I was a good listener, and I can also say, with all modesty, a good drinking companion.

I always knew I was in the presence of a great man, and I listened and learned. His knowledge was fabulous; no subject, philosophic or scientific, was beyond his ken, and his reading and knowledge of literature was astounding. He was the only man I ever met who had read Tolstoy's War and Peace *from cover to cover not once, but many times.*

I listened and learned. I learned more about literature and art, techniques of painting, and, most important, I learned more about the dedication and sacrifices that it takes to be an artist— an honest artist, that is—than anything I had learned in college or art school. Of course, we always exchanged choice bits of gossip about our friends, which added some spice and charm to our meetings. Yes, I learned many things from Burliuk, but unfortunately I learned only one word in Russian—the word for "bottoms up."

He was generous in his gifts of paintings to Lidia, myself, and our children. One of his last gifts to me—at a party on my 65th birthday—was a painting he called "Old Husband, Young Wife," showing a bedroom with twin beds, the husband aged and gray in bed reading a book, the young wife rosy and luscious standing at the foot of the bed. I got the point and stopped reading in bed.

David and Marusha Burliuk, two wonderful people who influenced both Lidia's and my life to an extent they hardly knew. They are both dead now. He died two years ago. She, in an appropriate gesture, died several months after he did. Lidia and I think and talk about them all the time. They are always with us and

will be. That is true immortality, don't you think? I hope some-
body writes about them soon, and when they do I hope they
write with love about love.

Chronology

1901   Born in Brooklyn, New York, February 17.
1915   Graduates, Public School 36, Brooklyn, New York.
1916   Attends Eastern District High School, Brooklyn, New York; Eron
        Preparatory School, New York City; Bedford Branch YMCA,
        Brooklyn.
1919–20 Attends Colby College, working as furnace tender, clothing sales-
        man, and dishwasher, to pay tuition and living costs.
1920   Enters Fordham University Law School, New York City.
1923   Graduates Fordham Law School, LLB; passes New York State
        Bar Examination, and is admitted to the bar of the state of
        New York.
1928   Marries Leah Schwartz.
1932   Visits France and Italy.
1936   Meets Alexander Dobkin and begins painting in his group.
1938–39 Studies painting with Yasuo Kuniyoshi.
1939   Wins scholarship award, American Art School, New York City.

1939–40 Studies painting with Sol Wilson.

1940   Spends summer in Mexico, studying work of Rivera, Siqueiros, and Orozco.

1941   Jury of Carnegie Institute chooses painting "Abstractionists" for "Directions in American Painting" exhibition.

Travels by tramp steamer to Panama, Ecuador, Peru, and Chile.

1942   Painting "Abstractionists," Phillips Memorial Gallery, Washington, D.C., "Trends in American Painting" exhibition.

Paintings "Back Street" and "Bargain Counter" selected by jury for "Artists for Victory" exhibition, Metropolitan Museum of Art. "Back Street" awarded 6th prize of $500 and is acquired by the Metropolitan Museum of Art.

1942–43 First one-man exhibition, Associated American Artists Gallery, New York City.

Invitation to hold one-man exhibition, Phillips Gallery, Washington, D.C.

Elected member of "An American Group, Inc."

Painting "City Carnival" acquired by Phillips Collection, Washington, D.C.

Appointed head of the art school for State, County, and Municipal Workers Union members.

1944   Exhibits "The Name is Walkowitz" in "100 Artists and Walkowitz" exhibition, Brooklyn.

Exhibits in "Pathways Through Art 1944," Puma Gallery, New York City.

Starts and conducts "Art in New York" interview program on art and artists on radio station WNYC, New York City.

Exhibits in "Painting in the U.S.A." at Carnegie Institute.

1945   Symposium, "Government Sponsorship of Art, Past and Future," with Holgar Cahill, Lynd Ward, and Bernard Meyers, Y.M.H.A., New York City.

Painting "Bravadoes" is acquired by Encyclopedia Brittania Collection of Contemporary American Art.

One-man show, Associated American Artists Gallery, Chicago, Illinois.

Elected vice president of the Artists League of America.

Exhibits in "Painting in the U.S.A.," Carnegie Institute, Pittsburgh, Pennsylvania.

Wife Leah dies November 25. Resigns State Insurance Fund.

1946   Exhibits in "Painting in the U.S.A.," Carnegie Institute.

Exhibits in "Contemporary Art in America," Kansas City, Missouri.

Exhibits in U.S. State Department show, Metropolitan Museum of Art, New York City.

Exhibits in group exhibition, Bothners Gallery, Johannesburg, South Africa.

Member of the Art Advisory Board, Encyclopedia Brittanica Collection.

Marries Lidia Brestovan, April 19.

1947   Exhibits in "Artists' Tribute to President Franklin D. Roosevelt."
Daughter, Lisa Kleinholz, born.

1948   Newark Museum acquires painting "The Name is Walkowitz."
University of Oklahoma acquires painting "Floral."
Auburn University, Auburn, Alabama acquires painting "Bank Nite."
Exhibits in "Painting of the Year," Pepsi Cola Exhibit.
Exhibits in "Society for Contemporary Art," Chicago Art Institute.
Exhibits in "La Tausca Exhibition," New York City.
Exhibits in "American Painting Today," Worcester Art Institute, Worcester, Massachusetts.
One-man exhibition, Associated American Artists Gallery, New York City.
Leaves New York for Paris with wife Lidia and infant daughter.

1949   Studies at the Grand Chaumière Academie Julien.
Works with lithographer Dorfinant at his studio on the Seine.
Works in etching with A. Moret, Rue St. Victor, Paris.
Produces a series of etchings and lithographs.

1950   Son, Marco Polo Kleinholz, born April 1 at the American Hospital, Paris.
Lives on the Isle de Brehat, Brittany, June to September.
Returns to the United States and studio on Seventh Avenue South, New York City, in September.
Jury accepts painting "Boy Meets Girl" for exhibit, "American Painting Today," Metropolitan Museum of Art, New York City.
Lectures, "Contemporary Trends in European Art," at Smith College, Northampton, Massachusetts.
Moves to Port Washington, New York.

1951   Exhibits in Fifth Annual Print Exhibition, Brooklyn Museum, Brooklyn, New York.
Exhibits in Library of Congress Ninth National Exhibition of Prints.
Exhibits in Carnegie Institute Invitational Exhibition of Prints.
Becomes Instructor of Fine Arts, Hofstra College, Hempstead, New York.

Exhibits in Hofstra College Annual.

1952 Painting "Close of Day" acquired by State of Israel.

Exhibits in Artists Equity Association, Founding Members Exhibition.

Receives Honorable Mention in Terry Art Institute National.

Exhibition of American Painting, Miami, Florida.

One-man exhibition, Associated American Artist Galleries, New York City.

One-man exhibition, Palmer House Galleries, Chicago, Illinois.

Traveling exhibition sponsored by the American Federation of Arts.

Exhibits in University of Illinois Annual Exhibition.

1953 Exhibits in National Academy Annual, New York City.

Wins first prize for painting, Manhasset Art Association, New York.

Exhibits, Pennsylvania Academy of Fine Arts 148th Annual Exhibition.

Travels to Mexico with Lidia.

1954 Exhibits in "Oils by 34 Jewish Artists," Jewish Center, Fairfax, Virginia.

Exhibits in "Twenty-nine American Painters," Montclair Art Museum, Montclair, New Jersey.

Group exhibition, "Drawing and Prints by Jewish Artists," Congress for Jewish Culture, New York City.

1955 One-man guest exhibition, North Shore Community Arts Center, Roslyn, New York.

Leaves with Lidia, Lisa, and Marco for a painting trip across the United States.

One-man exhibition, Associated Gallery of Art, Detroit, Michigan.

One-man exhibition, Palmer House Gallery, Chicago, Illinois.

1956 Commissioned to do triptych by Mr. and Mrs. Joseph Antonow, Chicago, Illinois.

Takes studio in Los Angeles with Morty Dimondstein, Arnold Mesches, and Marty Lubner.

Completes and installs triptych.

Returns to Port Washington, New York.

1957 Exhibits in "Fifty American Artists," Greenwich Gallery, New York City.

One-man exhibition, Palmer House Gallery, Chicago, Illinois.

Designs poster for Child Guidance Association, Great Neck, New York.

Exhibits in 22nd Annual, Butler Institute of American Art, Youngstown, Ohio.

1958   Engaged by Blankman Foundation with Alfred van Loen to paint and design an outdoor mural for the Sands Point Wild Life Preserve, Sands Point, New York.

One-man exhibition, Park Gallery, Detroit, Michigan.

One-man exhibition, Associated American Artist Galleries, New York City.

1959   Daughter Anna born May 7.

Exhibition and poster design for North Shore Child Guidance Association, Great Neck, New York.

Loan exhibition, Port Washington Public Library.

Exhibits at Butler Institute, Youngstown, Ohio.

Invitational Exhibition, Hofstra College, Hempstead, New York.

One-man exhibition, Park Gallery, Detroit, Michigan.

Marquette University, Milwaukee, Wisconsin, acquires triptych "Apple Tree, Apple Tree."

1960   Group exhibition, "Judaism in Art," The Village Temple, New York City.

Group exhibition, "Jewish and Biblical Themes," Har Zion Temple, Philadelphia, Pennsylvania.

Group Exhibition, Friendship Club, Moscow, Print "Boy and Bird" used for catalogue cover. Print acquired by Moscow Museum of Fine Art.

One-man exhibition, Park Gallery, Detroit, Michigan.

1961   One-man exhibition, Park Gallery, Detroit, on the theme "A Day in Coney Island."

Group exhibition, "Bible Themes," Village Temple, New York City.

1962   Designs and executes a series of prints for the White Winrock Hotel, Albuquerque, New Mexico. One-man exhibition held at the hotel in conjunction with opening ceremonies.

One-man exhibition, Galerie de Ville, Beverly Hills, California.

Exhibits in Pennsylvania Academy Annual, Philadelphia, Pennsylvania.

Exhibition, "Long Island Artists," Queens College, New York.

Ten prints acquired by the Port Washington Main Street School and installed in main lobby as a permanent collection.

One-man exhibition, ACA Gallery, New York City.

1963   One-man exhibition, Gallery del Sol, Fire Island, New York.

Lecture, "The Artist as Historian," Brandeis University, North Shore Chapter.

1964   Exhibition, Contemporary Prints, Mansfield State College, Mansfield, Pennsylvania.

One-man exhibition, ACA Galleries, New York City, in conjunction with the publication of *Frank Kleinholz, A Self Portrait,* by Shorewood Publishers, Inc.

One-man exhibition, Maxwell Galleries, San Francisco, California.

Exhibits in "Themes From Shakespeare," Harry Salpeter Galleries, New York City.

1965 One-man exhibition, Akron Art Institute, Akron, Ohio.

Akron Art Institute acquires painting "Housing Project."

Lecture, "The Artist and Contemporary Society," Park Synagogue, Akron, Ohio.

Travels to Rome, Italy, for one-man exhibition, ACA Gallery.

Print "Boy and Bird" chosen for UNICEF catalogue cover and 1965 calendar.

Retrospective exhibition, Nassau Community College, Garden City, New York.

1966 One-man exhibition, ACA Gallery, New York City.

One-man exhibition, Four Winds Gallery, Kalamazoo, Michigan.

Receives the First Annual American Artist Award by the Art Department of Nassau Community College, Garden City, New York. Award made in conjunction with the American Poets Festival honoring Emily Dickinson. The college acquires "Autobiography #1" for its permanent collection.

One-man exhibition, Galerie 99, Miami Beach, Florida.

Exhibits in "Protest Paintings U.S.A." at ACA Gallery, New York City.

1967 Moves with wife and family to Perrine, Florida.

Group exhibition, "Social Painters," ACA Gallery, New York City.

Exhibition, Joan Avnet Gallery, Great Neck, New York.

Group exhibition, Artist Equity Association, Bacardi Gallery, Miami, Florida.

1968 One-man juror, Florida Artists Group, University of Miami, Coral Gables, Florida.

One-man exhibition, Galerie 99, Miami Beach, Florida.

Receives honorary Doctorate of Fine Arts, Colby College, Waterville, Maine.

Commentator on art, radio station WIOD, Miami, Florida.

Conducts a series of lectures at the Lowe Art Museum, University of Miami, Coral Gables, Florida.

1969 (partial) Retrospective exhibition, Lowe Art Museum, University of Miami, Coral Gables, Florida.

One-man show, Galerie 99, Miami Beach, Florida.

Retrospective exhibition, Colby College Museum, Waterville,

Establishes the Frank and Lidia Kleinholz Scholarship at the Department of Art, University of Miami, Coral Gables, Florida.

114

Bibliography

1941   October 21, *New York Times*, Edwin Alden Jewel.
       October 23, *Pittsburgh Post Gazette*, Jeanette Jena.
       November, *Magazine of Art*, Forbes Watson.
1942   March 22, *Sunday Star* (Washington, D.C.), p. E6, Lelia Macklin.
       December 8, *New York Times*, p. 30, "Record Art Show."
       December 20, *New York Times* (Sunday), "Artists for Victory," Edwin Alden Jewel.
       December 23, *New York Times*, "Frank Kleinholz Holds Art Show," Edwin Alden Jewel.
       December 26, *New York World Telegram*, p. 5, "Kleinholz and Burliuk," Emily Genauer.
       December 27, *New York Times* (Sunday), art p. X9, Edwin Alden Jewel.
       December 27, *New York Herald Tribune*, Carlyle Burrows.
       December 30, *New York Sun*, Henry McBride.
       Catalogue foreword by John O'Connor, Jr., for first one-man show, AAA Gallery, New York City.

Artists for Victory, Metropolitan Museum of Art ("A Picture Book of the Prize Winners").

1943   January 1, *Art Digest*, "Kleinholz, Newcomer," Helen Boswell.

January 3, *Brooklyn Daily Eagle*, p. 18, A. Q. Kruze.

January 4, *Newsweek*, "Brooklyn-Born Gauguin," pp. 63–64.

May 10, *Times Herald* (Washington, D.C.), Jane Watson.

May 23, *Washington Star*, Miss Berryman.

September 19, *New York Times*, Howard Devree.

October 14, *Pittsburgh Post Gazette*, Jeanette Jena.

October 14, *Pittsburgh Sun Telegram*, Penelope Read.

October 16, *Cleveland News*, Louise Bruner.

November 23, *New York Times*, Edwin Alden Jewel.

1944   February 8, *New York Times*, p. 19, "Novel Art Display," Edwin Alden Jewel.

February 21, *New York Times* magazine, "Walkowitz 100."

February, *Magazine of Art*, "Sing Me a Song of Social Significance."

March 22, *New York Times*, "American Group Opens Art Show," Edwin Alden Jewel.

April 23, *Washingon Post*, Jane Watson.

April 25, *New Masses*, reproduction, "Window Cleaner."

April 27, *New York Times*, "Americans."

April 30, *Art News*, "Fine Words," etc., Margaret Breuning.

April, *Art News*, "The American Group" (reproduction).

May 9, *Pic Magazine*, feature article, Natalie B. Baker.

May 15, *Art Digest*, "20th Century Art Bought by the Encyclopedia Brittanica."

October 7, *New York World Telegram*, "They're Talking About," etc., Emily Genauer.

December 15, *Art Digest*, "Frank Kleinholz Scores With City Scenes," Margaret Breuning.

December 16, *New York World Telegram*, Emily Genauer.

December 20, *New York Times*, Edwin Alden Jewel.

December 24, *New York Herald Tribune*, Carlyle Burrows

December 24, *Pictures on Exhibit*, December, feature article on Frank Kleinholz by David Burliuk; Russky Golos, "New Works by Frank Kleinholz," reproduction, pp. 10–11.

1945   February, "Elizabeth McCausland discusses Picasso with Frank Kleinholz," reprinted by ACA Gallery.

March 18, *The Milwaukee Journal* (roto section, color review), "Bravadoes."

May 5, *New York World Telegram*, "Artists League Show," Emily Genauer.

December, *New York Times*, "The Whitney Annual Review."

December, *Art Digest*, "Kleinholz Finds a New Way of Life," R. F.

n.d. Reproduction, "Bravadoes," *Encyclopedia Brittanica Book of the Year*.

n.d. Symposium, "Government Sponsorship of Art, Past and Future" with Holgar Cahill, Lynd Ward, Dr. Bernard Meyers, Art Department YMHA.

1946   February 5, *New Masses*, "Artists on the Picket Line" (Kleinholz, Evergood, Gross, Pickens, Hirsch, Becker).

October 3, *New York Times*, "State Department Art Show Sponsor," Edwin Alden Jewel.

October 10, *Pittsburgh Sun Telegraph*, Penelope Reed.

October, *Contemporary American Painting*, published by *Encyclopedia Brittanica*, foreword by Donald Bear, pp. 67–68, "Bravadoes" reproduction.

October, *Art News*, "American Art Abroad," reproduced "Bank Nite." n.d. ACA publication, "Artists' Tribute to Franklin Delano Roosevelt," reproduction.

1947   January, *What's New* magazine (published by Abbott Laboratories), "Winter Sports," color reproduction.

October, *Art News*, pp. 17–18.

n.d. Publication *100 Jewish Artists*, published by YKUF Art Section.

1948   February, *Art News*, p. 30, T.B.H.

February, *Promenade Magazine*, p. 40, "Frank Kleinholz," Alfredo Valenti.

February, *Art News*, reproduction, "Rooftop View."

May 28, *New York Times*, "Two Group Shows," S. H. (Sam Hunter).

August 15, *New York Times*, p. 8X, Sam Hunter.

September, *Art News*, p. 9, "State Department Pictures Sold."

Sheldon Cheney, *Expressionism in Art*, rev. ed. 1945, p. 127, reproduction, "Spring is in the Air."

Natural Figure Drawing, by Anton Refregier, 1948, pp. 118–119, drawing, "Standing Nude."

1950   December 28, *Newsday*, "L. I. Barrister Shuts Law Books," etc.

1951   April 15, *New York Times*, Stuart Preston.

April 15, *New York Post*.

April, *Art News*.

December, *Carnegie Magazine*.

1952   February, *Art News*, p. 53, Henry McBride.

The Phillips Collection, p. 125.

Contemporary American Painting, University of Illinois, reproduced "Rendezvous," statement by Frank Kleinholz.

1955   February 27, *Chicago Sun Times*, review, reproduction, "Open Window."

March 20, *Chicago Sun Times*, book section, "Paul Gauguin," reviewed by Frank Kleinholz.

September 29, *Detroit News*, p. 44, "Brooklyn Gauguin," Joy Hakanson.

New York Times (Sunday), book review section, reproduction, "Boy Meets Girl."

New York Times (Sunday), book review section, "Street Crossing."

1956   *New York Times* (Sunday), book review section, reproduced "The Hikers."

1957   March 17, *Chicago Sun Times*, Sec. 3, p. 16, Frank Holland, reproduction, "View From the Palisades."

1959   March 29, *Detroit Free Press*, p. 8B, reproduction, "Walk in the Sun."

October 13, *Milwaukee Sentinel*, part 2, p. 1, "M.U. Given 3 Part $12,000 Set of Art Work Panels," Margaret Fish, reproduction, "Apple Tree, Apple Tree."

October 16, *Marquette Tribune*, p. 6, "Triptych Artist Writes About His Work."

October 28, *Roslyn News*, p. 24, "About Art," Saul Levine.

October, Catalogue foreword's "Frank Kleinholz" by Walter Yust, editor in chief, *Encyclopedia Brittanica*.

October, *School Arts*, pp. 33–34, "We Visited With Frank Kleinholz," "Why We Create," Louise Elliott Rago, reproduction "Birds Gotta Fly."

1960   *Philip Evergood*, p. 92, John I. H. Bauer, published by Frederick A. Praeger, Inc.

July 6, *Newsday* (Long Island), "Long Islander Finds Himself a Success as an Artist," p. 18, Bernie Bookbinder.

July 26, Catalogue cover for *American Group Exhibition*, Moscow, USSR, "Boy and Bird" by Frank Kleinholz.

August 8, *New York World Telegram*, Sec. E, p. B1, "An Artist *Inundated* at Coney Island," William Peper.

September 17, *Los Angeles Examiner*, "Too Old For Art?" by Carolyn Strickler, reproduction.

September 18, *Los Angeles Herald Examiner*, Alma May Cook, p. C3, reproduction, "Between Two Worlds."

October 17, *New York Times*, "Opening of Sands Point Wild Life Preserve."

October 18, *The Schreiber Times* (Port Washington, New York), p. 5, "Frank Kleinholz," Ellen Tibby, 3 paintings reproduced.

December 31, *Long Island Press*, "Frank Kleinholz," reproductions.

1962   January 3, *Newsday*, "Artistic Touch Brightens Long Island School Day," Alan Eysen, photograph.

1964   *Frank Kleinholz, a Self Portrait*, published by Shorewood Publishers, Inc., foreword by Philip Evergood.

January 17, *Port Washington Reporter*, p. 4, feature article.

January 25, *Great Neck Tribune*, pp. 1, 4, feature article.

January 26, *New York Herald Tribune* (Sunday), "About People," John Frogge.

January 28, *Newsday*, "Kleinholz Learns His Lesson Well," Virginia Sherwood, 2 reproductions.

February 8, *Long Island Post*, "Long Island Artist at ACA," reproductions, "Between Two Worlds" and "Bravadoes."

February 9, *New York Post*, p. 4, reproduction, "Bravadoes."

February, *Art News*, p. 16, review and reproduction, "Stop and Go."

March 2, *Publishers Weekly*, p. 114, review of *Frank Kleinholz, Self Portrait*.

March 26, *Port Washington News*, p. 4, "Presentation of painting Sea Gull by Frank Kleinholz," photograph.

June 21, *San Francisco Examiner*, V. 18, "Art," Alexander Fried.

June 22, *San Francisco Chronicle*, p. 43, "Big City, Big Sur," Dean Wallace.

June, *M.D. Magazine*, p. 252, reviewed book, reproduction.

July, *American Dialogue Magazine*, pp. 19, 20, "Abstract Art is Dead," dialogue with Ad Reinhardt, by Frank Kleinholz, reproduction, "Between Two Worlds."

1965   February 21, *The Plain Dealer*, "Brooklyn Gauguin Has Show in Akron," Helen Borsich.

March 7, *Akron Beacon Journal*, "Kleinholz Provides Comfortable Art," p. 23, Bernard Weiner, reproduction, "The Nest."

March 11, *American in Rome* (Rome), "Through a Key Hole," Maggi Vaughan, reproduction, "Forbidden Fruit."

March 15, *Newsday*, art page, "As the Romans Do," photograph of Frank Kleinholz.

March 17, *Voce Del Popolo* (Rome), reproduction and review.

March 25, *Le Settimana* (Rome), pp. 12, 13, review, photograph.

March 26, *Socialismo Democratico* (Rome), pp. 12, 13, review and photograph.

April 4, *Popolo 11* (Rome), review.

June 1, *Look* magazine, "Frank Kleinholz," story, photograph.

July 18, *Long Island Press*, photograph.

August 21, *The Plain Dealer*, "Brooklyn Gauguin Has Show in Akron," p. 10A, feature story by Helen Borsich, reproduction.

October 15, *The Denver Post*, p. 21, "Kleinholz Paintings on Display," Barbara Haddad, photograph.

October 22, *Rocky Mountain News*, p. 36, photograph of Frank Kleinholz.

December, *North Shore Community*, pp. 8, 9, feature article by Lesley Oelsner, 4 reproductions and 1 portrait.

"Boy and Bird," used by U.S. committee for UNICEF on catalogue cover and calendar.

Spring issue, *Colby Alumnus*, photo, biography.

Anrie Intermezzo (Rome), review.

1966   January 3, *The Miami Herald*, "Frank Kleinholz: Making a Simple Comment on Life," Doris Reno, photograph.

January 9, *The Miami Herald*, "Ex-lawyer 1-Man Opens Here," photograph.

January 16, *The Miami Herald*, p. 16, "On Music and Arts," Doris Reno.

March 6, *Kalamazoo Gazette*, "Kleinholz Story."

March 14, *Kalamazoo Gazette*, "Why Not? Exponent," Don W. Carlson.

September, *M.D. Magazine*, "The Fabulous Keyhole," p. 1, essay by Dr. Félix Martí-Ibáñez.

1967   June 8, *Newsday*, "Recent Kleinholz Works," etc., Jane Margold; reproduction, "Lovers in the Park."

October 10, *The Miami Herald*. Reproduction, "Jonquils."

October 29, *Miami Beach Journal*, p. 5, "What's Up in Art," Boris D. Paul.

The Ship in the Bottle, essays by Dr. Félix Martí-Ibáñez, p. 185, Clarkson N. Potter. Inc., New York.

1968   January 21, *The Miami Herald*, p. 2G, "New Ideas of Coloring, Style in Solomon, Kleinholz Shows," Doris Reno; reproduction, "Balloon Man."

January 28, *The Miami Beach Sun*, p. 5, Boris Paul; reproduction, "Let's Meet in the Park."

1969   (partial) March 7, *The Hurricane*, University of Miami, "Kleinholz Retrospective at Lowe," Alan Rose.

March 9, *The Miami Herald*, "Kleinholz Art at Lowe," color reproduction, "Young Artists."

March 9, *The Miami Herald*, feature by Larry King, "In Praise of Kleinholz."

March 14, *The Hurricane*, "Kleinholz' Art Exhibited."

Foreword to the catalogue of the retrospective at the Lowe Art Museum, by August L. Freundlich.

March 16, *The Miami Herald*, feature story, "Work Tells Painter's Amazing Story," Griffin Smith; reproduction of "Back Street" and photo of the artist.

April 6, *The Miami Herald*, review by Griffin Smith of exhibition at Galerie 99, Miami Beach, Florida.

A Partial List of Public and Private Collections

The Phillips Collection, Washington, D.C.
The Metropolitan Museum of Art, New York City
The Brooklyn Museum, Brooklyn, New York
Fine Arts Museum, Moscow, USSR
The Newark Museum, Newark, New Jersey
The Encyclopedia Brittanica Collection, Chicago, Illinois
Museum of Modern Art, Tel Aviv, Israel
Auburn University, Auburn, Alabama
University of Oklahoma, Norman, Oklahoma
Brandeis University, Waltham, Massachusetts
Marquette University, Milwaukee, Wisconsin
Butler Art Institute, Youngstown, Ohio
The Abbott Collection, Chicago, Illinois
Sewanaka High School, Long Island, New York
Syracuse University, Syracuse, New York

Port Washington Library, Port Washington, New York
Akron Art Institute, Akron, Ohio
Main Street School, Port Washington, New York
The Sackler Collections, New York City
The Joseph H. Hirshhorn Collection, New York City
Nassau Community College, Long Island, New York
The Blankman Foundation, Port Washington, New York
The Albert Dorne Collection, Westport, Connecticut
University of Miami, Coral Gables, Florida
North Shore Hospital, Manhasset, New York

Index

125

Design: BERNARD LIPSKY
Typography: SERVICE TYPOGRAPHERS, Indianapolis, Indiana
                Text type, *Aster*
                Display type, *Mistral*
Printing: LITHO ARTS, Inc., Miami, Fla.
Binding: NICHOLSTONE BOOK BINDERY, Nashville, Tenn.